DAY FO

D0292998

DAY FOUR

The Pilgrim's Continued Journey

Revised Edition

Robert Wood

UPPER
ROOM BOOKS®
NASHVILLE

DAY FOUR: *The Pilgrim's Continued Journey*
Revised Edition
Copyright © 2004 by Upper Room Ministries.® All rights reserved.

The Upper Room® Web site: www.upperroom.org

Cover design: Bruce Gore / Gore Studio, Inc.
Interior design: Nancy Cole-Hatcher
Fourth printing, revised edition: 2008

Library of Congress Cataloging-in-Publication Data
Wood, Robert, 1938–
Day four : the pilgrim's continued journey / Robert Wood. — Rev. ed.
    p. cm.
Includes bibliographical references.
ISBN 13: 978-0-8358-9880-5
ISBN 10: 0-8358-9880-6
1. Walk to Emmaus movement. I. Title.
BX8385.W34W658 2004
267'.1876—dc22

                                                                2003014648

Printed in the United States of America

CONTENTS

PREFACE

The intent of this book is to help you revisit your 72-hour Walk to Emmaus and discover its full meaning. I pray that your Emmaus experience has guided you to a deeper walk with Christ and a more fruitful servanthood in the ministry of your church. Your Walk to Emmaus lasted three days. The rest of your life will be a succession of Fourth Days. Emmaus challenges you to live Day Four as intentionally as the three days of the Walk, with a growing desire to become a willing and joyful servant of God.

The 72-hour Emmaus event did not begin your Christian pilgrimage. Much prayer and work went into preparing you to hear the message of Christ—the message of Emmaus. My sincere desire is that your continued ministry will be more effective in your church, your group reunion, and the Emmaus community as the Holy Spirit nurtures your discipleship.

Before your Walk to Emmaus, God's prevenient grace called you into a relationship with Jesus Christ. Your church, friends, and family all served as instruments of God's love. After your Emmaus experience, these same agents of God's love will continue to encourage you in your discipleship. The Holy Spirit will continue working in your life to perfect your servanthood. I pray that the message you heard during the Walk has caused you to become a more intentional disciple and that the group reunion effectively supports and strengthens you in your ministry and mission—joyfully being Christ in the world. If God is to be known in the world, Christians must become more intentional and fruitful in sharing the good news of God's love. Toward this aim, I hope you will read this book with the expectation of becoming more fruitful in your pilgrimage of faith.

Grace and Peace,
Robert Wood

1

HISTORY

The Walk to Emmaus is a program offering of The Upper Room, a section of the General Board of Discipleship of The United Methodist Church. In the truest sense, Emmaus is a spiritual renewal movement because it depends on each generation of pilgrims to pass on its enthusiasm to the next.

The Roman Catholic Cursillo movement greatly influenced the development of The Walk to Emmaus. The Cursillo (pronounced coor-SEE-yo) movement began in 1949 in the Roman Catholic monastery of San Honorato on the island of Majorca, Spain, out of a desire by some Christians to find spiritual renewal. The movement started out as a pilgrimage to the Shrine of St. James at Compostela, the great Spanish pilgrimage center of the Middle Ages. In the summer of 1948, the pilgrimage to St. James was directed by Father Sebastian Gaya and Eduardo Bonnin, the Lay Director. Father Juan Capo joined this group that would found the Cursillo movement.

The first Cursillo weekend in the United States was held in Waco, Texas, in 1957. Two Spanish airmen, who were in the States for flight training, and Father Gabriel Fernandez, a priest from Spain who had made his Cursillo weekend under the direction of the founder, had the responsibility of conducting this first American Cursillo.

The Upper Room held its first two model weekends for The Walk to Emmaus in Peoria, Illinois, in April and May of 1977 under the guidance of the Peoria Diocese Cursillo Community and its Spiritual Director, Father Thomas Henseler.

After developing the model and establishing a community in Nashville with the generous help of Father Charles Giacosa and the Nashville Cursillo Community, The Upper Room encouraged annual conferences in The United Methodist Church, Cursillo communities, and churches of various denominations to seriously consider this new, ecumenical model as a vehicle for renewing, enriching, and inspiring individuals to become more intentional disciples. Ecumenical Cursillo communities across the United States, sharing a common aim of church renewal, greatly aided The Upper Room in developing its ecumenical model. The model proved to be an effective tool in energizing disciples for ministry in local congregations, as well as a tremendous experience in sharing common faith in the Christian community.

In 1981, as the result of a mutual agreement between the National Secretariat of the Roman Catholic Cursillo movement and The Upper Room, The Walk to Emmaus received its name. Thus, The Upper Room Emmaus movement began its mission of equipping knowledgeable church leaders with a vital piety.

In the fall of 1984, The Upper Room took The Walk to Emmaus to Australia, thereby making it an international movement. The movement spread to the following countries:

- Brazil—1988
- Mexico—1989
- South Africa and Puerto Rico—1990
- India—1991
- Germany and Costa Rica—1992
- Zimbabwe—1993
- England—1995
- Ghana, Hong Kong (English speaking), and Estonia—1996
- Bulgaria—1997

- Cuba, China (Hong Kong—Cantonese speaking), and New Zealand—1998
- Singapore—2000
- Norway, Sweden, Dominica, and Switzerland—2001

By the end of 2002, an estimated 349 Emmaus communities had been established, with over 560,000 pilgrims attending a Walk.

Chrysalis, the youth/young adult expression of The Walk to Emmaus, began in 1984. In 1990 Chrysalis became an international movement when communities formed in Mexico and Australia. By the end of 2001, an estimated nine thousand Chrysalis events had taken place with some 300,000 youth and young adults in attendance.

The Upper Room maintains an International Emmaus Office in Nashville. An International Steering Committee advises The Upper Room staff to sustain a high quality throughout the Emmaus movement. The committee is comprised of representatives from four countries: Germany (1), Mexico (1), South Africa (1), United States (23–25)—one laywoman, one layman, and one clergyperson from each of five regions, three to five at-large members, and five ex-officio members. In 1997 The Upper Room added five regional field representatives in the United States who work part-time in shepherding new Emmaus communities, conducting board and community training, and organizing regional celebrations.

A book in the Emmaus Library Series, *The Early History of The Walk to Emmaus*, provides a picture of the first days of Emmaus and describes how the movement got started in Nashville. See Appendix 2 for more information.

2

BEFORE THE
WALK TO EMMAUS

Your Christian Pilgrimage

The Walk to Emmaus did not take place at the beginning of your Christian pilgrimage. Rather, the Walk is like coming into a movie that is already in progress. Most likely you made your Walk to Emmaus after having been a Christian for several years. There were, are, and will be many factors that contribute to your faithful living. Family, friends, congregations, special events, and ministry—all these have played a role in your Christian development. God has worked through a multitude of channels to share grace and love with you.

The call to love God and to serve with enthusiasm comes in the midst of many other demands and priorities. When God began speaking to you—through situations, friends, parents, a Sunday school teacher, or a pastor—you may have heard the message of God's love only faintly. God uses all sorts of ways to speak to you. Perhaps you grown more aware of your pilgrimage, but other priorities such as rearing children, establishing a career, or seeking pleasure took precedence, shelving or crowding out your relationship with God. Any relationship that is not given priority soon becomes meaningless if not lost altogether.

Although our yes to God's call is a sincere response to what we understand that call to be, it is not a once-and-for-all event. Because God's will is revealed slowly or gradually, there are always new beginnings, new calls to a deeper level of commitment. Our spirits are challenged again and again to deepen the relationship with God and to find fuller expressions of that relationship in meaningful ministries through the local church.

You can be certain that God has been reaching out to you in many significant ways. It is God's nature to love you and to seek channels like the church through which to share that love and draw you into a closer personal relationship. You may have missed those messages, but it is certain that God sent them.

Perhaps your previous pilgrimage included deep involvement in church life and in fruitful servanthood. Your Christian discipleship may have been a priority because you had heard and responded to the story of God's grace and the love God offers everyone. Your participation in educational classes, revivals, personal devotional disciplines, and ministry may have helped you grow spiritually. But perhaps after a while the weight of ministry became a burden. Maybe you remained duty-bound and obedient, but the joy of serving God had been extinguished.

You may also have found that you need confirmation of your pilgrimage's direction. We may be active in church and have our job, family, and ministry priorities in proper perspective, yet still we need affirmation that we are moving in the right direction in relationship with God. We feel that God is speaking to us, but is that voice the same one others hear? Or are we simply listening to the wind of our own minds? We find comfort when we see a road sign confirming that we are on the right road, headed in the right direction.

All this is to say that people come to The Walk to Emmaus with a variety of needs, having traveled many roads in their pilgrimages of faith. Rarely will you find people at the same place in their faith who have arrived there by the same route. It is equally true that no two persons will be at the same place after the three days of common journey during The Walk to Emmaus. There is no prescribed expectation of what someone will be like once having made a Walk. A successful Walk is one in which participants spend three days in the company of other pilgrims experiencing God's love and forgiveness and receiving encouragement to be more faithful disciples and to share that same love with others who need to hear the message of reconciliation.

It is important to understand that the church, the body of Christ in its many manifestations, nurtured you to the point where you could hear and receive the message of The Walk to Emmaus. The church will continue to care for your spiritual needs and shape your life of servanthood following your three days. The Walk to Emmaus is not a new denomination or an ecumenical parachurch that one joins in hopes of finding a perfect corporate life. It does not take care of all one's spiritual needs or direct all of one's ways of serving God. The Walk to Emmaus is a spiritual renewal movement that has been called to a unique task *within* the church. Anytime a person views The Walk to Emmaus as more valuable than active participation in a local church, that person needs to take a hard look at his or her motives and regain a proper perspective.

Let's use this analogy. If people decide they need a continuing education course to help them in their business, they do not give up their business to become perpetual students. Regardless of how meaningful and enlightening the course is, the purpose of taking it is to *help* them in their business, not to become their new business. The same is true of The Walk to Emmaus. It does not intend to become your new business, new church, new lifeline, or new anything. It is meant to be just one experience toward your becoming a saint in street clothes, mediating God's love and compassionate forgiveness to others.

One of the unique aspects of The Walk to Emmaus is that it asks you to give your undivided attention for seventy-two hours. When was the last time you gave your church—or for that matter, anything—your undivided attention for seventy-two hours? Many situations could be changed if a person willingly devoted seventy-two hours of concentrated attention to them. Quality time changes things.

Now in your Fourth Day, you may want to spend some time putting your Christian journey into perspective. It may help to write down crucial points in your faith journey, draw a map of your journey, make a collage, or simply to spend time reflecting upon your pilgrimage in silence. You may want to talk with someone about where you felt your journey had been headed before your Walk. Memory is a vital factor in who you are. Events in your life have created memories, and those memories can help you chart the course for the rest of your life. Memories make an imprint, help you interpret, give meaning to every other experience you encounter. Spend some time recalling memories of your faith journey, the people and events that helped you decide to accept Jesus Christ as your Lord and Savior. Familiarize yourself with the bank of memories from which you draw, consciously or unconsciously, to interpret every experience that comes your way. You may need a friend or spiritual guide to help you. Or this recalling of memories may be something you have done many times before and feel comfortable doing by yourself. Whatever the process, take time to put your Walk to Emmaus in perspective with the rest of your faith journey.

3

THREE DAYS IN THE COMPANY OF FELLOW PILGRIMS

Experiencing a New Testament Community

It is impossible to describe *your* three-day Walk to Emmaus. Just as each of the four Gospels gives a different account of the life and ministry of Jesus, each person who attends Emmaus has a unique experience. Many events during your three days were unplanned and unexpected but were God-guided and appropriate. With insight, Christians can learn to recognize the difference between a humanly motivated and a God-initiated experience. This chapter shares the intent— divinely guided—behind the movement called The Walk to Emmaus.

The book of Acts gives a vivid account of the early Christian community. These people met constantly to hear the apostles teach, to share a common life, to break bread together, and to pray. A sense of awe was evident, and many marvels and signs were brought about through the apostles. Those whose faith had drawn them together shared everything; they sold their property and possessions and made a general contribution as the need of each person required. Like-minded, they remained faithful to daily attendance at the Temple, and they shared meals with unaffected joy as they broke bread in one another's homes. As they continually praised God and enjoyed the favor of all the people, day by day the Lord added to their number.

This is a remarkable account of the early Christian community. In the three days of The Walk to Emmaus, the Emmaus community hopes to provide you with an experience of a loving community of people trying to be like that early church.

A friend brought you to The Walk to Emmaus. A sponsor is asked to bring you to the weekend as a matter of love. The sponsor prayerfully considered how best to become an instrument of God in offering you the gift of love called The Walk to Emmaus. Prayer is an essential part of preparation for this event, and your sponsor prayerfully asked God to lead each step of the way as he or she invited you to attend your Walk. Most people have a certain amount of uneasiness about a new venture; careful preparation on the sponsor's part can greatly reduce anxiety about the new venture of Emmaus. Remember the importance of preparation as you recruit your friends to attend a Walk. Emmaus is a gift of love—you want to give it to someone you care about deeply. And, unlike a Christmas gift, with The Walk to Emmaus you may tell the recipient exactly what he or she will receive.

As the weekend unfolded, your response depended more on your openness than on the content being presented. When persons approach the Walk with an open, positive attitude, they predictably find it to be a positive experience. Likewise, when persons come to The Walk to Emmaus with a closed mind, a self-satisfied attitude, or a sense of being pressured, they may benefit little from it. Proper preparation encourages participants to anticipate that God has something beautiful in store for them, and they will be eager to learn, grow, and spend time with other pilgrims in joyful Christian fellowship.

On your Walk to Emmaus, the first night's silence offered a focused time to search out your own attitude and examine your relationship with God. Examining your relationship with God through Jesus Christ gave you a chance to determine your intentionality in your journey of faith. You had an opportunity to discover where being a faithful servant to God's claim on your life fit into your list of priorities. This process involved soul searching on your part to determine how important The Walk to Emmaus really was for you to give three days to it. You were asked to consider this question: What has your interaction been with the man Jesus? In answering that question truthfully, you received some idea about the place of faithful service to God in your priorities.

If you had a sleepless night, it may have had less to do with sleeping arrangements than with where you were on your faith journey. It may help to take some time now to reflect on your priorities and see exactly where on that list is your personal statement "I am a Christian."

The meditation on the first morning introduced the day's theme of God's love and grace. Each talk, act, gesture—even silence—became a gift of love. Of all the messages you receive in your life, the affirmation of God's love is the most healing and nurturing. The leadership team and the Emmaus community, while human instruments, were sincerely willing servants who conveyed this message of God's love. Your reception of that love, of course, depended upon your willingness to receive it. The greatest defense a person has against receiving love is to blame the one attempting to love him or her. If someone finds it hard to receive another person's love, he or she may find it equally hard to receive God's love, particularly when it comes in human form. That person may dictate to God the terms for being loved: "God, if you love me, surely you want me to have a big house, a fine car, an important job." Because many persons are accustomed to expressing love through things, they expect God to express love that way too.

Because The Walk to Emmaus is a human instrument, you experienced instances of being loved through things. The gifts of agape, even though they symbolize love and sacrifice (God's kind of love), may have appeared to be just so many bookmarks and posters bought at a Christian bookstore. Some of us are still perfecting our way of loving. Yet, we are all a part of God's kingdom, which includes novices as well as saints.

A later chapter will cover the content of the talks during the weekend, but it is important to point out here that the talks and the experience go hand in hand. The mental, emotional, spiritual, and experiential message is the same: God loves you.

As the first day unfolded, you began to learn that many persons were carrying out kind deeds for you behind the scenes. People were praying for you, preparing food for you, and sacrificing for you through fasting and special acts of agape—reinforcing the message of God's prevenient grace, God's loving you even before you knew it. You began to feel this love, and the talks reinforced this understanding of God's love.

These three days provided a brief encounter with a New Testament community. They were geared toward creating a desire in you for such a community and toward equipping you with skills to help move you to a life filled with God's grace, one full of prayer and servanthood.

For more information, see the Emmaus Library Series, specifically the book *What Is Emmaus?* by Stephen Bryant.

4

THE MESSAGE
OF EMMAUS

Those Fifteen Talks and More

During The Walk to Emmaus, the conference room team presented a short course in Christianity. The talks did not necessarily contain concepts new to you. You probably had already learned many of these ideas in Sunday school classes, heard them preached from pulpits, read them in scripture, and recognized them as part of the Christian tradition. However, during The Walk to Emmaus the ideas were presented as a carefully structured course in which you—with undivided attention—learned about the depth of the Christian life.

The team asked you to take notes during the talks so that after the weekend you would be able to review the material you heard. This chapter helps you reconsider the message of Emmaus and see the interrelationships and deeper meanings of the talks and meditations.

The first night of silence provided a chance for you to reflect on where you were on your journey of faith. Then the rhythm of the short course began.

The LOVING FATHER/PRODIGAL SON meditation introduced the theme for the first day—the love and grace of God. The meditation continued the theme of introspection. The Spiritual Director asked you to put yourself into the parable to discover which of the characters most closely reflected your own life. You may have been the lost son or daughter in a strange country desiring the husks being fed to the pigs. Perhaps you recognized yourself as the loving parent hoping that a wayward child would come home. You may even have been the son or daughter who stayed at home but did not enjoy the company of a loving parent, seeing the relationship only as duty. Were you, and are you today, like the prodigal son after he came to his senses—desiring to be at home with God? Each of us desires to be at one with God, and our spirits will not rest until we find that at-homeness. Again, the parable heightened your awareness of where you were on your faith journey.

The rhythm of the presentations was designed to allow you to reflect on the depth of your commitment. First, one of the speakers presented a message and you were given a few moments of silence to reflect on how you had experienced this message in your own life. Next, the small group at your table discussed the content of the talk so that each of you could put your experiences in perspective with others. Then your group was asked to summarize its discussion, prioritizing the main points and gleaning basic truths. Finally, you joined with others at your table to draw a poster, write a song, or perhaps create a skit illustrating the major points of the talk as your group experienced it. This allowed you to move from the intellectual side to the creative side of your brain and to internalize the content of the talk in a different way.

The first talk of the day, PRIORITY, posed one major question: Do you have a priority for your life? The talk challenged you to rise above the animal world, where natural instinct rules, and to become a complete human being, capable of setting priorities for your life. You heard the speaker explain that by choosing priorities you set the direction of your own life. The PRIORITY talk did not present a new discovery or unfold a theological concept. It simply addressed the question of setting priorities. It started right where you were as you came to the Walk. For example, you made attending the weekend a priority. You may have had to take time off from work to attend, and you had to spend time away from your family. Maybe you had to forgo a shopping trip or a golf game to attend the three-day event. In fact, all who attended your Walk had made a priority of spending three days in the company of people they didn't know, sleeping in strange surroundings, and, in some cases, feeling uneasy about what might happen.

The second talk, PREVENIENT GRACE, directly addressed the theme of the day—God's grace. While the first talk called you to be a human being, the second talk called you to be a Christian human being. It encouraged you to consider whether you had made the life of faith a top priority. In this talk, the speaker helped you discover some of the ways God had loved you and wooed you into a relationship even before you were aware of it. This talk pointed out that the very nature of God is to love you, and God loved you even before God got your attention. This talk did not focus on your response but on how freely God loved you even without a response.

The third talk, PRIESTHOOD OF ALL BELIEVERS, attempted to explore the meaning of the church. The first talk called you to be a human being; the second talk called you to be a Christian human being. This third talk called you to be a Christian human being in community. In such a community, Christians invest in one another's lives and hopes in order to work out God's grace in the world. They provide mutual support and demonstrate compassion for one another. This sense of support allows them to shoulder the burdens of individuals in a hurting world.

The fourth talk, JUSTIFYING GRACE, examined how individuals respond to God's offer of a relationship, which you heard about in PREVENIENT GRACE. While the earlier talk focused on the relationship God offers, JUSTIFYING GRACE focused on your acceptance of that relationship. Keep in mind that these are not different kinds of grace but different ways of understanding the love God gives us. God loved you before you were aware of God's love. For God's love to have meaning and to grow, you must accept and respond to it for the relationship to be complete. Your relationship with God is justified by faith—a growing trust you place in God and through which you accept God's will for your life.

The last talk on the first day, LIFE OF PIETY, summarized the total message of the day. It presented the lifestyle of a person trying to live a life in grace (the Christian life lived in and through God's grace). Through LIFE OF PIETY, you learned how to give your heart to God. Having chosen the best priorities for your life, having understood how much God loves you, realizing that a community of people will travel with you on your journey of faith, and responding to God's love through faith, you discipline yourself to live a life in grace—a life of piety. The life of piety is a life full of God's grace.

The message of the first day was the grace of God. Each talk, while focusing on different themes, helped you understand how God's grace works and how you could be a more fruitful person by opening yourself to God's grace.

At the conclusion of the first day, you were given time to examine your conscience and evaluate whether you had given yourself entirely to the Emmaus weekend. This examination was offered not just as an exercise but as an experience to be repeated regularly for spiritual health. The examination of conscience served as a reminder to give yourself fully to your Walk, to keep these three days from slipping away from you and being wasted. The last talk of the day presented an authentic Christian lifestyle—a life of piety in which your whole life is directed toward God.

The second day of Emmaus is often called the Jesus Day. The morning meditation, FOUR RESPONSES TO CHRIST, provided four scriptural accounts of ways people responded to Jesus. You reflected on your own response to him—and considered how to make a full, authentic response to Jesus Christ. It was not assumed that you had never made a response to God's love, but all of us need opportunities to move deeper into our commitment to the Christian life. The meditation set the theme for the day: Jesus models a faithful response to God's grace.

The first talk on the second day was GROW THROUGH STUDY. In LIFE OF PIETY you learned how to give your heart to God. In

GROW THROUGH STUDY you learned about giving God your mind. The talk pointed out that a mature Christian is an informed Christian—informed about the mind and heart of God by knowing the scripture. A Christian knows about the world and its needs and works toward gaining the best insights on how to alleviate the hurting world's agonies. Human beings rise above the animal world of simple instincts when they become knowledgeable and use that knowledge to help build God's kingdom. Study, like piety, can be approached in an intentional, systematic way, resulting in a deeper relationship with God and empowered Christian discipleship.

The next talk, MEANS OF GRACE, presented the many channels of God's grace and helped you understand how and why the Christian community celebrates those sacred moments. This talk took a close look at baptism, Communion, confirmation, marriage, forgiveness, healing, scripture, and prayer—and it pointed out how believers receive God's grace through all of these avenues. Immediately after the MEANS OF GRACE talk, a Communion service took place, giving you the chance to experience the healing power of God's grace in your own "dying moments"—moments of dying to the pain of sin and receiving the gift of God's grace.

The third talk on the second day, CHRISTIAN ACTION, completed a trilogy with LIFE OF PIETY and GROW THROUGH STUDY. In this talk you learned that a tripod of piety, study, and action supports the life in grace. In your personal piety you give your heart to God; in your study, you give your mind to God; and in CHRISTIAN ACTION, you are challenged to give your hands and feet to God in loving service. This talk was designed to help you discern what God is calling you to do in response to the gift of God's grace, love, and relationship. You learned that Christian action is your response to God's love, not a way of winning it.

The next talk, OBSTACLES TO GRACE, introduced a cunning acquaintance—sin. This talk pointed out that at times the adversary may deceive us into thinking that we are still on the journey when in truth we may have been diverted at an enticing rest stop. This talk helped stimulate awareness of the fact that all of us put up barriers to the relationship God offers us. It addressed the obstacles to our relationship with others and our true self in Christ. Finally, it offered solutions for overcoming these obstacles through the cross of Jesus Christ so that we may respond fully to the relationship God offers each of us.

The last talk on the second day, DISCIPLESHIP, summarized how the speaker had attempted to live the life in grace, becoming a disciple of the loving God. The speaker pointed out that as you grow through study, celebrate God's grace in your life, become involved in Christian action, and overcome the obstacles to grace, you indeed become a modern-day disciple. Discipleship is a lifestyle of living your faith to the fullest, and it becomes a total response to Jesus Christ as both Savior and Lord of your life.

The Candlelight service is an integral part of the short course on Christianity. Having had Jesus Christ presented as a model for your living, you were given an opportunity to make the specific response of a deeper commitment to God through Jesus Christ. During Candlelight you were introduced to the Emmaus community—brothers and sisters in Christ who had been supporting and would continue to support you in your commitment.

The third day, the Sending Forth Day, began with the meditation THE HUMANITY OF JESUS. As Christians, we are well aware that Jesus' death on the cross has assured our death-defeating resurrection and promised eternal life. This talk pointed out that by your response to this meditation, by understanding and assuming the human qualities of Jesus, your life can become informed and reformed. The speaker stated that by knowing the human qualities of Jesus, you can learn how to use or control your own natural abilities and traits—such as empathy, anger, love, and understanding—to become more Christlike. This meditation set the tone for the day, preparing you to transform everyday events in your life through the presence of Christ and to move toward establishing the reign of God in your daily environment.

The first talk on the third day, CHANGING OUR WORLD, explored ways you can evaluate the environment in which you live and set priorities to transform your world. By taking an honest look at self, family, community, and vocation, you can become aware of the difference Christ makes and how you can bring Christ into these environments. Through the use of examples, the speaker challenged you to have a plan for bringing Christ into your world. Of course, such a plan is never simplistic because life is not simplistic. The adage "Make a friend, be a friend, and bring a friend to Christ" was offered as a focus for this plan. You were encouraged not to fear the magnitude of the task; you need only identify some simple first steps to establishing the kingdom of God where you live.

The next talk, SANCTIFYING GRACE, helped you understand the source of power needed for the plan outlined in CHANGING OUR WORLD. You were introduced to the ways in which you can move deeper into your relationship with God. In SANCTIFYING GRACE you looked at the work of the Holy Spirit—perfecting in you the ability to choose God above all other relationships in your life. You learned that your life, moving toward perfection, requires discipline and an open willingness to serve God and to be Christ in the world. To accomplish this, devotional disciplines are essential. You would not become a good golfer or cook or musician without practice. Through the devotional disciplines, you practice and claim the presence of God and make yourself available for God's renewal of the world. Growing in grace is not an option for a Christian; it is your baptismal vocation.

The third talk on this final day was BODY OF CHRIST. The apostle Paul, in many of his letters, refers to the body of Christ as that community of faithful servants willing to be ears, hands, and feet by which the message of God's love is conveyed to all of God's people. This talk provided a third look at the call and ministry of the church. You learned that you are a more effective instrument when you work toward being Christ in the world by cooperating with other Christians. In community we support and challenge one another to live the life in grace and serve with compassion.

The PERSEVERANCE talk introduced the tool that allows you to keep alive the encouragement you experienced during the Walk— the group reunion. This dynamic group helps you persevere in being a disciple. The group reunion provides strength, support, and challenge in being intentional about your discipleship. During The Walk to Emmaus you were a part of a small table group that helped make the event more meaningful for you. Over the three days you grew together and in essence formed and experienced a group reunion without knowing it. The table discussions helped clarify your thinking, broaden your perspective on issues, and challenge you with new ideas. Participation in a weekly group reunion (which probably will be made up of persons other than those with whom you shared your weekend) extends this experience beyond the Walk and strengthens your pilgrimage of faith.

The last talk, FOURTH DAY, gave practical guidance for your journey in faith beyond the short course in Christianity presented in the Emmaus Walk. The speaker addressed the group reunion's value in supporting his or her journey of faith. He or she also stressed the importance of community gatherings, serving on board committees, team training, and participation in Emmaus weekends as additional means of keeping alive the fire of the Walk.

Several subtle but vital messages occurred during the weekend that do not come under the heading of a talk, but these messages are of equal value to the talks. The first message is *the involvement and partnership of laypersons and clergy.* Each layperson and clergyperson on the conference room team plays a vital and distinctive role during the three days. No individual is more important than another but at all times should complement and help build the environment so that pilgrims are encouraged to find new levels of commitment and appreciation for their developing discipleship. In fact, what this partnership hopes to accomplish is a model for how clergy and laity can work together in building the ministries of the local church. Each member of the team, both clergy and lay, plays an essential role, resembling members of the body Paul writes about in 1 Corinthians 12:12 and following. Some are called to be eyes, some feet or hands, but all are called to be part of a larger entity, the body of Christ. The manner in which laity and clergy work together during the weekend sets a tone for cooperation in the local church. Emmaus is not a lay movement but rather an expression of the church at work in the spiritual renewal of its members.

The clergy do have the unique role of being Spiritual Directors. This role calls them to the task of providing sensitive and scriptural guidance to pilgrims during their discerning moments over the course of the weekend. You can find a full explanation of this role in the Emmaus Library Series book *Spiritual Directors.*

Another subtle message of the weekend is *the role of music.* With the help of Elise Eslinger, the Upper Room staff examined how music can enhance and reinforce the spoken message of the fifteen talks and four meditations. They made every effort to ensure that music on each Walk supports the talks or prepares pilgrims to hear the full message of the spoken word. Each solo serves as a continuation of the message that precedes or follows it. Music for The Walk to Emmaus should never be viewed as performance but instead as an attempt to color the air surrounding pilgrims. For a full explanation of the role of music, see the Emmaus Library Series book *Music Directors.*

Third, the message of *prayer* is critical to Emmaus. The entire weekend is wrapped in prayer. Prayer takes place before the first team member is chosen and before each team meeting. Prayer is offered before each talk, asking the Holy Spirit to make up for anything lacking. Prayer is offered in the chapel, the conference room, and the dining room—in fact, around the world—that pilgrims will receive God's message of love, forgiveness, and hope. Rather than being an afterthought, prayer is an integral part of Emmaus because it is an essential part of each Christian's life. Emmaus hopes to kindle in each pilgrim's life the desire to pray more frequently and fervently in all aspects of life.

Finally, another unspoken message of the Emmaus weekend is *servanthood.* Acts of servanthood undergird the entire weekend. Whether the act is cleaning the restrooms, letting someone go first through the doorway, serving meals, or offering a cold drink of water, these acts display God's love. God brought about the salvation of the world through the great sacrifice of God's Son. Emmaus attempts to move pilgrims toward understanding that sacrifice through acts of servanthood; it also reinforces the idea that many lives are brought to that salvation through the sacrifice of others. Early Christians were identified by the way they loved each other. Jesus modeled servanthood on the night before his crucifixion when he washed the disciples' feet. Emmaus seeks to follow in the footsteps of Jesus by emphasizing acts of servanthood, thus modeling for pilgrims a quality they should seek to incorporate in their own faith journeys.

Remember that the whole reason The Walk to Emmaus exists is to make you a more faithful disciple, an active church member, and one who seeks every opportunity to express faith in loving acts of servanthood.

5

AGAPE

God's Message of Love

The affirmation of God's love is the most healing and nurturing message you will ever receive. Why, then, is it sometimes so difficult to accept God's love personally? One reason may be the understanding and experience we bring to the word *love*. We use the word so casually that it has lost much of its original meaning. A great deal of the power of love is obscured by the shallowness of the relationship it describes. It is little wonder that we greet the message of God's love for us with skepticism.

The Greeks used three words to describe three distinct relationships, all of which we translate as love. A look at these Greek words will help us distinguish between the love we may have experienced and the love we receive from God.

The first—*phileo*—describes a kinship type of love—the love that exists between parent and child, between brothers and sisters, or between close friends.

The second—*eros*—describes conditional love based upon attraction or personal benefit. We could call it, "I will love you . . . if you love me . . . if you are attractive to me . . . if the relationship will benefit me in some way."

The third—*agape*—describes unconditional love—love that is freely given and unrelated to our deserving it or earning it. It is a self-sacrificing love that reflects total commitment to the one who is loved. The night he was betrayed, Jesus emphasized the significance of the agape relationship by declaring that the greatest expression of love is to lay down one's life for another.

The most evident way to lay down one's life for another is to die for that person. All of us have heard of heroic incidents in which one person sacrificed his or her life in saving another. When asked if we would willingly die for someone else, we probably would answer yes to the hypothetical question. Sacrifice seems more comfortable on a hypothetical level—when we are reasonably sure that the situation will never present itself to us. If, however, we limit our understanding of laying down our lives for another to such literal expressions, we remove ourselves effectively from a deeper understanding of sacrificial love—agape. Few of us are called to die for another, but all of us are called to sacrificial love on a daily basis. That daily sacrificial love—the life in grace—is the essence of The Walk to Emmaus. Agape is truly laying down our lives for others. Such sacrificial love is no less heroic in its daily expressions than in its ultimate expression, death.

Agape is the kind of love God has for each of us—the love you felt during your Emmaus weekend. Coming face-to-face with agape in the lives of Christians can move us to the point of conversion. When we experience acts of agape on our behalf, we begin to move toward accepting God's love for us personally. When people, with all their human courage and frailties, love us with sacrificial, unconditional love, we catch a glimpse of the depth of God's love for us. That is the purpose of the seventy-two hours—to help you begin to accept how very much God loves *you*.

The first act of agape you experienced during your weekend began long before your arrival at the site of your Walk. Your sponsor prayed to become an instrument of God's love in your life by sponsoring you. Prayer is an important act of agape, a means of bringing the grace of God into another's life. Constant prayer undergirds all that goes into The Walk to Emmaus.

The acts of agape continued as your sponsor talked with you about The Walk to Emmaus, submitted your application, obtained agape letters for you from your family and friends, arranged for your transportation to the Emmaus site, and perhaps even took care of your home responsibilities to free you to concentrate on the weekend. These and other acts of agape by your sponsor represented a loving sacrifice of time and energy on your behalf in order that you might feel more deeply God's love for you.

Your sponsor wasn't the only one sacrificing on your behalf during your Walk to Emmaus. The entire Emmaus community became involved in bringing God's love to you. Loneliness in the midst of a confused, crowded world plagues every human being. We need the supportive, caring touch of others to put the stamp of authenticity upon us—to let us know we are loved. God created us for community; without it, we are restless and incomplete.

The Walk to Emmaus brings a new awareness of community. At first, it cracks the walls people have built around themselves, chipping away at the rubble in their lives, until finally, the overwhelming awareness of God's love for them breaks over them like a wave—acting as the birth water that ushers them into the life in grace. Once bathed in the caring, loving sacrifices of others, Emmaus pilgrims have the sincere, ongoing support of the Emmaus family for encouragement as they take seriously the priority of a life wholly directed to God. When you received your cross on Sunday afternoon, you were commissioned with the words "Christ is counting on you." Christ is counting on you as a person living the life in grace to support and encourage others as they experience the reality of God's love in their lives.

Agape is the word the Emmaus movement uses for this process of supporting one another. However, our brothers and sisters in the Cursillo movement use *palanca*, a Spanish word meaning "lever." Prayer and sacrifice become the lever that moves persons closer to God. Agape also serves as a lever, helping remove obstacles from people's lives that prevent them from discerning and accepting God's grace. Prayer and sacrifice on their behalf give people a glimpse of God's grace in action in the lives of others. These actions show that the life in grace is possible and that a supportive community of Emmaus pilgrims will help along the way.

Now that you have completed your Walk to Emmaus, you will have many opportunities to help make God's love visible to persons seeking it. Perhaps the most obvious way is to serve on an Emmaus team or help in the kitchen. It is easy to think that once the team is chosen and the kitchen help is recruited, the weekend is taken care of. Despite the importance of these responsibilities, they are only a small part of the agape that goes into the Emmaus weekend. You may not serve on the team or head up the kitchen, but you still are needed. The Walk to Emmaus is truly a community activity—it takes many people to make a weekend possible: team members, kitchen helpers, prayer volunteers, participants at Candlelight and Closing, luggage carriers, and helpers to set up the facility. This does not take into consideration all the table-agape makers, cake bakers, letter writers, and cleanup crew.

The following list includes acts of agape that make The Walk to Emmaus possible, including pre-Emmaus and post-Emmaus activities. As you can see, you can offer agape in many ways that will allow others to actively experience God's love in their lives. Your participation will vary with each Emmaus weekend.

SPONSORSHIP: Do you remember how much your Walk to Emmaus meant to you? It would not have been possible without the prayer and sacrifice of your sponsor. Sponsorship carries with it many responsibilities, and it is a critical factor in the effectiveness of The Walk to Emmaus. You can share God's love with someone you know by sponsoring that person during an Emmaus weekend. Chapter 8 examines the responsibilities of sponsorship.

PRAYER: Prayer begins when you consider sponsoring someone, continues during the weeks of team preparation, and undergirds the entire seventy-two hours. The 72-Hour Prayer Vigil means that there are 144 half-hour slots of time to be filled for each weekend. Members of the Emmaus community are encouraged to come to the prayer chapel at the Emmaus site to pray, but when that is not possible, they pray wherever they are—at home, at the office, while shopping, in the car, at traffic lights! Prayer undergirds the entire Walk to Emmaus and is a vital part of the continuing life in grace. If for some reason you cannot participate in an Emmaus weekend in other ways, this opportunity for agape is especially suitable. Through prayer, you continue to offer agape on behalf of those making their Emmaus Walks wherever you happen to be.

SNACK AGAPE: During the three days of the Emmaus weekend, snacks such as cookies, fruit, cheese and crackers, and vegetables and dip are provided during breaks for the pilgrims. Food has traditionally been considered an expression of love and fellowship—perhaps you will choose to offer agape in edible form for an upcoming Walk to Emmaus.

GENERAL AGAPE: Remember all those letters that were read during your Emmaus weekend, then posted on the walls to be read and reread until you finally began to realize that people you had never met were making sacrifices for you as an expression of God's love? Some of the persons wrote that they were praying for you throughout the weekend. Others may have chosen to attend special worship services on your behalf, while still others chose to fast for a meal or even more throughout the seventy-two hours that you were making your Walk to Emmaus. Remember the colorful and clever banners that brightened the walls during the weekend, reminding you that God loved you personally?

Now you have a chance to make your love visible and offer your own sacrifices on behalf of pilgrims making a Walk to Emmaus. Dates of Emmaus weekends are posted on The Upper Room Web site (www.upperroom.org); select the Emmaus icon and follow the prompts. The agape chairperson is listed with an address. Many requests for agape come from other countries. This is another opportunity to offer your acts of agape on behalf of persons seeking to live the life in grace, growing ever more aware of God's love for them.

CHAPEL AGAPE: Members of the Emmaus community gather to pray in the chapel while each talk is being given during the Emmaus weekend. They offer prayers on behalf of the pilgrims, that their hearts will be open to the message God has for each of them; and on behalf of the speakers, that God's love will be clearly visible in them as they give their talks. This expression of sacrificial love, both for pilgrims and team members, is another way to manifest God's love and help move persons closer to the life in grace.

KITCHEN AGAPE: Jesus' life and ministry clearly offers a model of servanthood. Although he was God, Christ put aside his majesty and walked among us as a servant rather than as a king. Cooking and serving meals during the Emmaus weekend is a big job, and it takes many hands to carry out this task successfully. Helping in the kitchen expresses God's love, a self-sacrificing love that generously spends itself on behalf of others. Perhaps you will choose to offer agape by volunteering to help in the kitchen during an Emmaus weekend.

SEND-OFF, SPONSORS' HOUR, CANDLELIGHT, AND CLOSING: These times are vital in the life of the Emmaus community and in the lives of those making their Walk to Emmaus. At these times, new pilgrims glimpse the family they are joining, and they witness the life in grace to which they are being called. Participation in these events is a joyful opportunity to offer yourself as agape on behalf of others, and all members of the Emmaus community are encouraged to attend.

PERSONAL AGAPE: The agape letters given to pilgrims are priceless. Their value lasts long after the Emmaus weekend has ended. In many cases, the prayers and sacrifices expressed in these letters have been life-changing. Your letters to persons making their Emmaus Walk serve as expressions of God's love at work on their behalf. As a sponsor, your efforts to secure these personal agape letters is a vital part of surrounding your candidate with God's personal love. Remember, though, that giving gifts during the weekend is not appropriate. If you wish to give the person you are sponsoring a special remembrance of his or her Emmaus weekend, do that after the weekend. Personal agape distributed during the Emmaus Walk is limited to letters.

TABLE AGAPE: A seemingly endless variety of gifts appears on the dining tables beginning with the Friday evening meal. These offerings of agape are provided with loving prayer and concern by members of the Emmaus community. In many instances, they represent hours of prayer and preparation by persons and group reunions in anticipation of upcoming weekends. Table agape is offered as a symbol of God's continuing love, and it often serves as a reminder of the Emmaus event long after the weekend ends.

You have many opportunities to offer acts of agape during a Walk to Emmaus; this book hasn't touched all of them yet. Often persons attending from out of town need transportation; baggage must be carried up and down stairs, and the Emmaus site must be set up and taken down each time.

You may have noticed that all of these expressions of agape occur within the three-day Walk to Emmaus itself. Yet agape is not limited to the Emmaus weekend or even to the Emmaus community as a whole. Offering acts of agape—sacrificial love—on behalf of others so that they may move closer to accepting God's love for them is a significant part of the continuing life in grace. Take some time to look around you—at home, at work, in your community. What situations provide you the chance to offer acts of agape to others? Some Emmaus pilgrims choose to volunteer in an inner-city soup kitchen, while others organize to do repairs on the homes of elderly persons. Emmaus pilgrims, both individually and as group reunions, volunteer to visit inmates in local prison systems, and some serve as tutors for inner-city children. The opportunities are endless and unique to your environment. Prayerfully consider where you may offer self-sacrificing love to those around you.

Having considered all these aspects of agape, we still aren't quite finished. It would be foolish not to admit that an Emmaus weekend is most often a hectic time. Coming to the chapel to pray isn't always convenient. Getting up at 3:00 A.M. for your slot in the 72-Hour Prayer Vigil requires discipline. Send-Offs, Sponsors' Hours, Candlelights, and Closings sometimes conflict with activities you would rather be doing. Your mind may suddenly go blank in the middle of writing an agape letter. You may realize with dread that you haven't the slightest creative idea for table agape. These things happen to everyone at one time or another.

Because we are humans with many layers of self-interest to overcome, it takes time to learn how to communicate agape to others. This is an integral part of growing in the life in grace. It takes time to mature in our understanding of sacrifice and to refine our expressions of sacrificial love. One dictionary defines *sacrifice* as "offering something precious to God." In offering acts of agape to others, we need to grow in our understanding of and willingness to sacrifice. Sacrifice implies that we are offering something personal and precious—we are offering ourselves in a very real way. Consider your choices for acts of agape carefully. Do you dash into a Christian bookstore at the last minute to buy bookmarks and call that agape, or do you buy the bookmarks ahead of time and write a prayer for each pilgrim on the back? Are you planning ahead to prayerfully write personal agape letters to the pilgrims or to make table agape that will remind them of God's love after the Emmaus weekend, which requires a sacrifice of time and an investment of yourself? Or are you offering agape that requires an investment only of your money?

As you grow in your understanding of God's sacrificial love for you, you will mature in the ways you express that sacrificial love to others. Likewise, when you make the effort, the *sacrifice*, God's grace becomes more abundant in your life as well. You are blessed far beyond what you have given. There is a joy in knowing that you have placed others before yourself and that through your acts of agape they may come to know God's love for them and live the life in grace.

6

GROUP REUNION

Keeping the Fire Alive and Your Nose to the Grindstone

Many aspects of our world threaten to destroy the life that The Walk to Emmaus presents—the truly Christian yet truly human life. Once we return to our everyday world, it does not take long to discover that living the Christian life alone is practically impossible. One way of tapping into God's power to make an authentically Christian life possible is through contact with other Christians who share the priority of a life in grace. The Christian life is strengthened and deepened by being shared. However, contact with other Christians does not mean just any contact; it means contact particularly with Christians who share the vision of a life directed wholly to God through Christ. During The Walk to Emmaus, the PERSEVERANCE talk introduced the concept of the group reunion as a way of maintaining that kind of contact—an important means of persevering in the life in grace.

Throughout The Walk to Emmaus, you learned that a life in grace means living a life wholly directed to Christ. You learned that piety, study, and action are the legs that support a life in grace. You also learned that you cannot achieve this life on your own; you must have the right support to accomplish it. Unfortunately, if your group reunion's shared activities are not Christ-centered, they can lead you away from Christ.

Scripture contains many stories of fellowship. Christ chose twelve disciples to accompany him, and he sent them out two by two to witness. Interestingly, he told them they didn't need to take money, food, clothing, or even shoes with them. They already had the one thing they needed above all—one another's support along the way.

The New Testament calls this special fellowship *koinonia*—fellowship among those who share a common knowledge of Christ and want to grow in that knowledge by sharing with others in a life in grace. In Acts 2:42 Luke states, "They devoted themselves to the apostles' teaching and fellowship, to the breaking of bread and the prayers." That is what you did during the Emmaus weekend and what you need to continue to do in order to live the life in grace.

Remember that The Walk to Emmaus is just one part of your life in grace. The whole weekend is directed toward the hope that once you have experienced this Christian ideal, you will meet in special Christian communities and share how Christ is working in your life. These special communities are called group reunions. The group reunion is one of the greatest treasures of the Emmaus movement. It helps you persevere in the life in grace and hold on to those valuable aspects of the weekend when you return to your life in the world. The group reunion serves the life of the Emmaus community.

Just what is a group reunion? Basically, it is made up of two to six persons who meet once a week at a regular time for about an hour. The group reunion may include persons you met during your weekend, your sponsor, or other pilgrims you know. It may even incorporate persons who have not made a Walk to Emmaus but are seeking to direct their lives wholly to Christ. The group meets at a time and place convenient to all the members—in a home, an office, a room at your church, or even a restaurant. Any convenient place with privacy and a comfortable atmosphere will work. The setting and meeting time do not matter as much as the regularity with which you meet—regular attendance is the strength of the group reunion.

Group Reunion Card

Once you have formed a group, the reunion card gives a format for remaining focused on your life in Christ. The structure of the group reunion is valuable only when people are looking for the means to accomplish what they want—to live and grow in the life in grace encountered during the Emmaus weekend. Just as holding a hammer is a major obstacle to using your hand unless you actually want to hammer something, your group can become an obstacle to its members. A common reason for unsuccessful groups is that people participate without wanting to accomplish the purpose of the group reunion. With this in mind, let's look at the group reunion card.

The meeting begins with the Prayer to the Holy Spirit, which focuses attention on Christ's presence and seeks God's guidance for growing together in the life in grace. This prayer sets the tone of your time together as being intentionally in contact with Christ.

Next, the group reviews the service sheet—the center portion of the card. This exercise helps members examine their piety, study, and action over the past week. They share briefly with one another any significant happenings in each of these areas of the life in grace. At times, you may have a lot to share about your spiritual journey; at other times, you may have nothing to share. Reviewing the service sheet helps you gain a picture of where you are at that particular time in your walk with Christ. It will be clear if your life in grace is balanced in regard to piety, study, and action or if you need to focus more on one area or another. By sharing your significant insights and experiences with other group members, you contribute to their spiritual growth as well as your own. By sharing your failures, you can draw strength and encouragement from one another to continue your journey. By sharing your plans for the coming week, you enter into an accountability that will help you grow in your life in grace. Review the service sheet carefully and seriously. To keep this process from becoming routine, enter into it with a searching heart and glean from it the nurture it was designed to give.

After each person has reviewed the service sheet, begin discussing the following subjects.

CLOSEST TO CHRIST: A great deal of comfort can be gained from looking back over the past week and identifying the moment when you felt closest to Christ. As you make this exercise part of your ongoing spiritual journey, you will become more and more sensitive to Christ at work in the world and in you. Some of your moments closest to Christ will be ones in which Christ's presence bursts upon you unexpectedly and with great joy; at other moments, you may realize Christ's presence as a comfort in the midst of trouble or sorrow. As you grow in awareness of Christ's continuing presence in your life, you will also become more aware of God's abiding love for you.

CALL TO DISCIPLESHIP: At what moment during the past week did you feel you were responding to God's call to be a disciple? The overarching message of The Walk to Emmaus is that God loves you personally. As followers of Christ, we are to help others become aware of and accept God's great love for them. In what ways did you help move others closer to Christ at home, at work, and in your community? In what ways did you make God's sacrificial love visible to someone else? You will answer the call to discipleship in some ways simply by being yourself. Other calls to discipleship require planning and organization if significant areas of our society are to reflect God's love and justice. Be sensitive to the range of ways in which you may be called to discipleship as part of your life in grace.

DISCIPLESHIP DENIED: When was your faith tested this week through failure? Your first inclination may be to identify when during the past week you received a call to discipleship that you ignored. This question, however, has a deeper focus. When you take your life in grace seriously and respond to what you perceive to be a call to discipleship, you may be disappointed to discover that in spite of your careful planning, your action fails. Perhaps someone rejects your overture of friendship; perhaps a plan for community action fails because you cannot gain enough support. While such times can be demoralizing, they can also strengthen your faith. You cannot predict or control the outcome of your discipleship; you are accountable only for responding to the call. Failure to achieve a particular goal in response to discipleship is no excuse for apathy; it is a challenge of faith to leave the results of your efforts to God.

YOUR PLAN: It has been said that if you fail to plan, you plan to fail. Outline your plan for your piety, study, and action for the coming week, and share it with the members of your group. Planning makes your spiritual growth intentional rather than accidental, and sharing your plan with your group provides an accountability based upon mutual concern for one another.

GROUP REUNION ACTIVITIES: Group reunions provide an excellent support base for acts of agape, both within and outside the Emmaus community. You may decide to volunteer to help in the kitchen for one or more meals during an Emmaus weekend. Your group may want to spend part of its meeting working on table agape for upcoming Walks. Some groups study together, choosing a resource suitable for small groups on a topic that will nurture the life in grace. Still others volunteer for community service projects. As you continue to meet and grow together, you will become increasingly aware of occasions for agape. Keep in mind, however, that these activities are in addition to the review of the service sheet rather than being a substitute for it. If time is a factor, review the service sheet before entering into other activities. You may choose to meet at a separate time to work on table agape or service projects, keeping intact the time for sharing your spiritual journeys.

PRAYER FOR SPECIAL NEEDS: Before closing your meeting, take time to share special needs and pray about them together. These needs may be personal, or they may be concerns of a larger scope. Praying for one another strengthens the bond of the group reunion and nurtures a growing intimacy. This is also a good time to pray for members who are unable to attend. Make it a priority to recall those needs in prayer throughout the week.

PRAYER OF THANKSGIVING: End your time together with the Prayer of Thanksgiving, calling to mind that the purpose of your life in grace is to draw ever closer to God.

These times together in your group reunion will become precious to you. The group reunion provides a setting in the hectic round of everyday living where you can gather for support, affirmation, and guidance in living your life in grace. You are not alone; you have joined together with other Christians for strength. And, with Christ as the center of your relationship, you can persevere!

Criteria for Forming Group Reunions

There are four criteria for forming group reunions:

1. Group reunions are based on friendship.
2. You must make the effort to start or join a group; there is no imposed formation.
3. Every participant contributes; there is no group leader.
4. Groups can change.

First, your group must be made up of people you really want to be with. When members genuinely enjoy one another, they can help one another grow in the life in grace. This does not necessarily imply that you should choose a group in which everyone agrees with your viewpoint on every issue. Exposure to a variety of viewpoints and personal experiences enriches the spiritual journey and helps one grow and mature in the faith. However, to achieve the depth of intimacy and sharing needed to be significant spiritual friends, the group reunion should be comprised of persons who genuinely love and respect one another.

The second criterion relates to the first. It might be easier to form groups from the persons at a particular table during an Emmaus weekend or from persons who live or work in a specific area, but often the approach that takes the most effort is the one that produces the best results. No one will arbitrarily place you in a group reunion. You must look for one and join on your own efforts as a result of your own commitment to growing in the Christian life. The Emmaus community will assist you in finding a group reunions, but the responsibility for becoming a member of a new or existing group is yours.

Third, each member takes responsibility for the group process. There is no leader or chairperson. No one will call you to remind you to come to the weekly meeting. No one will lead the group when it meets. Members share the responsibility for meeting with the group each week and participating as a group in acts of agape. There is no specified leader, but rather a group, the members of which share a common commitment to one another and to growing in the life in grace.

The fourth criterion is vital. If a group doesn't seem to be working out for you, by all means begin or find another one. You may need to change groups for any number of reasons, but you never outgrow your need to belong to one.

Characteristics of an Effective Group Reunion

Effective group reunions share five characteristics:

1. Earnestness
2. Sincerity
3. Discretion
4. Regular attendance
5. Confidentiality

For your group reunion to become Christ-centered and Spirit-empowered, each member must take it seriously. Your participation is crucial. The group must meet together regularly and be willing to risk openness and honesty with one another, knowing that whatever is shared will be held in confidence. What is said in the group reunion stays there. Confidentiality builds trust among group members and enhances the Christian life. When your group has these characteristics, you experience the strength and stability of Christ-centered fellowship—true *koinonia*.

7

EMMAUS

An Instrument of the Church

The sole purpose of the Emmaus movement is to strengthen disciples within the ministry of individual congregations. Emmaus, in partnership with the church, inspires leaders to become more effective and intentional in their ministry. Emmaus is neither competitive with nor a substitute for your own church. Although The Walk to Emmaus is a unique and powerful instrument through which faithful people are renewed and inspired, it cannot provide the well-rounded programs that an individual congregation offers, such as education, evangelism, missions, and stewardships. In short, Emmaus does not intend to become anyone's "new church."

However, Emmaus does have a unique role in the church's task of nurturing strong, committed disciples who compassionately serve Christ in the world. The unique role of The Walk to Emmaus is spiritual renewal. The first distinctive component of this renewal experience is the content—the short course in Christianity presented during the fifteen talks of the weekend. Given by laity and clergy, these talks are a mixture of information and personal experience. The speakers tell how they have absorbed the message of Christ, had their lives formed by it, and lived it in their journeys of faith. Although each speaker has the major responsibility for developing his or her own talk, the total team, during the team-building process, works toward developing cohesive, unified presentations that carry the single message of God's active grace in the world. In addition, prayer and Holy Communion form an integral part of the team building and preparation for the short course in Christianity. As a result, the pilgrims hear the good news in a way that is uninterrupted by other thoughts, influences, and activities.

The average Christian who attends worship and Sunday school each week spends about as much time in one year hearing the gospel of Jesus Christ as one person spends attending The Walk to Emmaus. Put another way, The Walk to Emmaus concentrates a whole year of church participation into an intensive seventy-two-hour experience. The Walk offers the additional advantage of consistency of thought and absence from the world's agenda. For these reasons, you were asked not to permit phone calls, television, newspapers, or business matters to interrupt your focus on becoming more intentional about your faith pilgrimage.

The second component of The Walk to Emmaus is the pilgrim's experience of a New Testament community. The table groups become friendship groups that experience a new revelation in communication that is possible for committed Christians. The table group prays together, which deepens Christian relationships. After spending seventy-two hours with a group of pilgrims, we cannot help but grow in our understanding of intimacy. The experience of support by the Emmaus community through prayer and acts of service and sacrifice helps us grow in understanding the unmerited love of God.

The third component challenges pilgrims to reappraise their priorities and to consider a deeper commitment to discipleship in all of their environments—home, job, community, and church. The first talk challenged you to rise above the world of instinct and intentionally set priorities in life. Subsequent talks helped you grasp the understanding that the primary priority is God's grace—a vital and loving relationship with God.

Last, and this may be the most distinctive component, The Walk to Emmaus strongly encourages pilgrims to find a small group of friends who will spend time in weekly group reunions supporting and challenging one another to become more fruitful disciples in Christ's church. It has been said that an isolated Christian is a paralyzed Christian. To be effective, every disciple must be supported and challenged by other disciples of Jesus Christ. People function best in community; this characteristic is part of human nature. Belonging to a group reunion fulfills one of our basic needs—to find and experience a deep level of trust with others and to willingly invest ourselves in one another.

Each pilgrim takes away from the weekend three essential thoughts: piety, study, and action. Following the three days he or she must constantly ask where God may be trying to use him or her in ministries of piety, study, and action. Here are some helpful questions for pilgrims to consider: Has God gifted you in one of these areas, and can the church use your gifts in building effective ministries in worship, Sunday school and other studies, or in the social application of faith? Has God given you the gift of discernment to use in the church's efforts to help the poor? Has God given you the gift of insight and speaking so that you can become an effective and dynamic teacher in your church's education ministry? Has your gift of support been encouraged during this weekend so that you can offer that support to the pastor and lay leaders of your church? Has prayer moved you so much during these three days that you would like others in your congregation to share that experience? Might God be asking you to organize a prayer group in your church or among your friends and family?

These are basic experiences of the Christian community and will be a part of any church program. Emmaus exposes pilgrims to these experiences in a dynamic fashion through a well-prepared team in a setting uninterrupted by other agenda or demands. In a sense, the Emmaus experience builds on all the groundwork provided by the pilgrim's own church experiences, but it provides an "over the top" or "mountaintop experience" that is sometimes hard to achieve amid the demands of family, job, and community.

Likewise, a vital church life following The Walk to Emmaus is essential for pilgrims' fellowship, nurture, and direction for ministry to continue. Emmaus cannot become a new church for pilgrims. The church needs to be sensitive to ways it can help renewed Christians serve most effectively within the congregation. If the church is unresponsive or unreceptive to persons with a new enthusiasm for their faith, the results may be disastrous. Sometimes persons change so dramatically after The Walk to Emmaus that they wonder why the church did not provide them with this experience before. They must remember that the church provides The Walk to Emmaus as an expression of the church at work, the body of Christ renewing its members.

The church need not be defensive that someone else is interfering with its business. The Walk to Emmaus is a part of the body of Christ. Made up of faithful members of Christ's churches, it seeks to renew the local church. At the same time, congregations must be receptive to renewed Christians and must be creatively resourceful in putting these people to work in vital ministries of the church.

This process makes several assumptions about the church:

1. It is an active body involved in vital ministries where disciples can be fully employed in the name of Christ;
2. Laypersons are part of the church's decision-making structure;
3. The pastor has a vital interest in a spiritually renewed laity;
4. The church understands the unique roles of lay and clergy and how they can work together;
5. It knows how to identify and coordinate the gifts of its members to obtain maximum unity and effectiveness;
6. The church firmly believes that the kingdom of God can be established in the lives of individuals, through which a community of believers will arise who corporately celebrate in Christian worship.

Simply put, the churches that benefit the most from Emmaus are those churches that are receptive to the work of Emmaus and know how to involve renewed members in their ministry.

The efficacy of The Walk to Emmaus depends on individual congregations knowing how to use the program. Emmaus is not a place where the local church sends its "problem members" to get them straightened out, nor is it an evangelistic tool to make new Christians. Emmaus strengthens church leaders, building on the nurture and care the church has already begun. During those seventy-two hours, The Walk to Emmaus cannot do everything; instead, it focuses on the spiritual renewal of church leaders. Keep this in mind when seeking out new pilgrims for The Walk to Emmaus. *The sole purpose in recruiting pilgrims should be to strengthen our own congregations.*

The church can offer unique ways to build upon the Emmaus experience by helping new pilgrims become intentional about evangelizing their families, work, community, and church environments. Congregations can help Emmaus pilgrims benefit from the small-group experience by finding ways to make this an integral part of their programs. At best, the church will not be threatened by the Emmaus experience but will embrace it as an extended ministry of the community of the faithful and accept it as a partner in the demanding task of bringing the kingdom of God into the grasp of searching Christians. *Coming Down from the Mountain,* a book in the Emmaus Library Series, can help you understand some of your feelings after your Walk to Emmaus.

8

≈✠≈

THE NEXT GENERATION

Being a Good Sponsor

The strength of any Emmaus community is a direct result of the community's recruiting practices. If the community makes a commitment to recruit strong church leaders for the purpose of strengthening the local church, then the community will be a strong, vital force in the renewal movement. If, on the other hand, The Walk to Emmaus is looked upon as a hospital where every human illness can be cured, it will weaken the entire community. Emmaus is designed to spiritually renew church members who, in turn, can Christianize their environments. The church is a vital part of this renewal effort. If strong church members are recruited to attend Emmaus Walks, the Emmaus community will provide authentic spiritual renewal.

Another overriding purpose of Emmaus is to Christianize environments such as home, business, friendships, and churches. As people consider the reorientation of their priorities, experience the grace of God in a loving community, are wooed by the Holy Spirit to be disciples, and participate in a supportive group following the weekend, they naturally will want to transform the most significant areas of their lives as a result of this new experience of love.

Here are several qualities to look for in prospective pilgrims. First, they are already on a pilgrimage, willing to grow and move forward in their journeys of faith.

Second, persons should have a Christian orientation—no, a Christian *fervor*. They know God can make and has made a difference in their lives. Third, prospective pilgrims are not so consumed by other situations that they will not be able to give full attention to the message and experience of The Walk to Emmaus during the seventy-two-hour experience and all the follow-up activities.

When you find a prospective pilgrim, follow these suggestions:

STEP 1: Pray. Focus your prayer on how this person can become a more vitally alive Christian in helping bring God's kingdom into his or her natural environments rather than on how you can get this person to attend an Emmaus weekend. Rather than thinking about the weekend for a prospect, envision a new vitality of faith that will last a lifetime. When you have a focus on God's call for ministry for this person, then move to the next step.

STEP 2: Make an appointment. Casual conversation about your Emmaus experience may help, but if you are serious about asking someone to become a part of the Emmaus community, make an appointment to talk to him or her. If the person is married, pay attention to both husband and wife; do not recruit one person and expect him or her to recruit the spouse. Extend a personal invitation as a means of enriching faith and thus become more effective disciples. Inform each prospective pilgrim that there are many ways to enrich faith but that you have benefited from the Emmaus experience.

STEP 3: Issue the invitation. After sharing your own experience, make sure the person knows that your invitation is to a more vitally alive relationship with Jesus Christ, not just to attend a weekend. The three days are part of a whole new way of life. Carefully explain the group reunion, community gatherings, service on board committees, team membership and formation, and renewed interest in serving one's church. Don't overwhelm the prospect by making him or her feel that the invitation is to full-time ministry, even though, in a sense, that is the invitation. Help the person understand that with God's love and grace, every aspect of life will change for the better.

STEP 4: Encourage the commitment. Take a registration form with you and ask the prospective pilgrim to fill it out in your presence so you can answer any questions. If the person is married, get an application from the spouse at the same time. Then complete the back of the form and mail it to the registrar, along with the registration fee.

STEP 5: Continue to prepare. You're not finished—just beginning. Continue to pray for and stay close to the person to answer any questions that may arise. Start collecting agape letters and letting friends know that he or she is going to attend a Walk to Emmaus, enlisting their prayers. If the person's pastor has not attended a Walk, you will want to explain The Walk to Emmaus to the pastor and enlist support and prayers for your pilgrim. Help the pastor start visualizing how this spiritually renewed person can serve in the ministry of the church.

STEP 6: Handle the pilgrim's weekend responsibilities. If the person has a family, attend to the members during the weekend. The team will take care of your pilgrim. Continue to pray and attend Send-Off, Sponsors' Hour, Candlelight, and Closing, but at other times give the pilgrim space to make his or her own Walk.

STEP 7: Remember Day Four. After someone has attended a Walk, don't forget him or her. Spend some time together, helping the pilgrim digest the experience. Give direction to the pilgrim's newfound enthusiasm about being a disciple. Help the pilgrim take those first new steps of discipleship in the right direction so that no one becomes alienated from the person or from The Walk to Emmaus. Make sure your friend joins a group reunion. If you are not currently in a group reunion, go along. Bring the pilgrim to the first Emmaus Gathering following the Walk.

STEP 8: Go back to the church. Make sure the person returns to church with an enthusiastic, supportive attitude. Again, if the pastor of the church has not attended a Walk to Emmaus, take time to talk about the experience and explain the pilgrim's new enthusiasm for ministry. Directing this new enthusiasm requires sensitivity.

STEP 9: Understand Emmaus. Help the person understand how he or she can serve the Emmaus community. Talk about signing up for the Prayer Vigil, serving in the kitchen, volunteering agape for the tables and for snacks, serving on board committees, and serving on teams. Entry into serving on Emmaus teams is through the servants' entrance.

STEP 10: Help the pilgrim sponsor someone else. When pilgrims you have sponsored consider recruiting someone for The Walk to Emmaus, they will probably recruit the same way in which they were recruited. Help them discern which people would respond to a weekend of love and thus become more vitally alive disciples in their homes, communities, vocations, and churches. Help them with all ten steps the first time through.

A good experience during The Walk to Emmaus can be ensured when one goes with the proper attitude. A good attitude comes from knowing what to expect. Here are some suggestions on how to prepare your prospective pilgrim.

Things You Must Tell a Pilgrim

1. If you are talking to married persons, keep in mind that equal commitment to the Walk from both members of a couple is desirable. Don't rush decisions, but let a couple work toward a common understanding of what the two expect The Walk to Emmaus to do for them.

2. Sleeping arrangements differ in each location; explain as thoroughly as possible what they will be. Sleeping and showering are personal activities, and participants need to know how to prepare for these during The Walk to Emmaus. Also explain how meals will be handled so that persons on special diets can make the necessary arrangements to continue their diets during the Emmaus weekend.

3. Let the person know that participation is expected in all activities from 7:00 P.M. on Thursday until 7:00 P.M. on Sunday. Free time is limited to about three and a half hours during the weekend, and if the group gets behind in the schedule, free time is diminished.

4. Everyone should bring his or her own bedding, pillows, towels, washcloths, and comfortable clothes, including clothes appropriate for free time, which might include hiking, sports, or exercise. Impress on the pilgrim the relaxed nature of The Walk to Emmaus—no dress clothes are necessary.

5. Inform the pilgrim that except for emergencies, he or she should not expect contact with family or business during the weekend.

Things You Will Want to Tell a Pilgrim

1. Tell the person what the three days meant to you and how the Walk affected your personal relationship with Jesus Christ.

2. Tell how the Walk has affected your family, church, job, and community.

3. Tell how Emmaus has helped you change your priorities.

4. Tell how you sustain the spirit of the Walk through group reunions, gatherings, and serving during subsequent Walks.

5. Tell how each weekend is unique, but each person seems to find exactly what God wants that person to experience. The pilgrim can look forward to gaining a new enthusiasm for serving God.

Things You May Want to Tell a Pilgrim

1. Fifteen presentations will take place during the weekend, dealing with subjects like setting priorities, how to improve your knowledge about God, how to serve God in everyday settings, how to be a disciple, and how to persevere in faith.

2. Small groups spend time discussing these presentations.

3. Time is spent in the chapel meditating and praying.

4. Communion is emphasized. Tell the person about your response to the Communion services.

5. There is plenty of good food, fellowship, and a chance for all persons to find what they need for a life in Christ. Participants should expect to deepen their relationships with Jesus and to renew their enthusiasm for serving Christ.

Things You May Not Want to Tell a Pilgrim

1. The Candlelight service has its own special effect in showing God's love, and you may want that to be a surprise.

2. The personal agape letters cannot be described adequately since you do not know what each person will write. You may want them to be a surprise too.

3. Don't try to anticipate what someone will get out of The Walk to Emmaus. Simply tell your own story. There are *no* expected results other than experiencing God's love.

It is extremely difficult to avoid recruiting persons we want to see changed. But when we recruit persons with this motive, we are recruiting from the standpoint of wanting others to become like us. We are comfortable with who we are as Christians, and we want everyone else to be like us so that we will be comfortable with them. *No one should be recruited to attend The Walk to Emmaus to be changed into our own image of what a Christian should be like.* Rather, we should recruit a variety of Christian perspectives so that the complexity and beauty of God's personality taking form in human beings can be seen. The primary reason for recruiting someone to attend a Walk to Emmaus is to deepen that person's relationship with Christ and to create an enthusiastic disciple to work in God's kingdom. Your primary motivation for recruiting a person ought to be Christ's love in you wanting that same love for the prospective pilgrim. Building the kingdom of God is serious work, and building a strong Emmaus community is part of that task.

The Emmaus Library Series has a book on sponsorship. See Appendix 2 for ordering information.

9

A FINAL WORD

A growth process takes place within the Emmaus family, just as it does within the church family. God has many things in store for us and wishes to reveal them to us. Those first seventy-two hours of Emmaus do not provide nearly enough time for God to share all that God desires for us to know and experience. Therefore, as a pilgrim continues his or her life within the Emmaus community, God will stretch the individual for the task of ministry ahead. I have always said that I witness greater growth in a person as that person serves on teams than I did when the person was a pilgrim. In a sense, as a person serves on a team, he or she is in the limelight for a brief time (about twenty-five minutes if giving a talk) and then gets to settle back into the journey of being a pilgrim for the remainder of the weekend, waiting to see what God has in store.

Immerse yourself in prayer and see what God has in store for you. Be willing and ready to share yourself, but also be ready to receive what the humblest pilgrim may offer you. You never know where or when you may see the face of Christ. God's blessings come at unexpected times and in unexpected places. God has never exhausted the last opportunity to tell you that you are loved. Put yourself in the position to hear and feel that message. You will never be disappointed. You can never outgive our abundant God.

Be open to the serendipitous life God wishes to share with you.

The Walk to Emmaus has much to offer disciples in their growth process and their kingdom-building efforts. There will be moments of comfort, support, and challenge. The journey never ends. But I am convinced that among the Emmaus family, just as is true among the Christian family, one can find the finest individuals to be traveling companions in the search to find God's will and to live within it. They will pray with you, comfort you, and challenge you to find God's kingdom and share that kingdom with others. It is my prayer that God will bless you richly through the Emmaus experience.

De Colores!

APPENDIX 1

GLOSSARY

As you participate in the Emmaus movement, you will want to be familiar with terms that are part of the weekend experience and its ongoing life. This brief glossary is provided to help you grow toward better understanding and more meaningful participation.

AGAPE ACTS: Special acts of prayer, sacrifice, and expressions of Christian love on behalf of a pilgrim by another Christian or a group.

CANDLELIGHT: A special service held on Saturday night as an act of prayer and sacrifice on behalf of the pilgrims attending the Walk. The entire Emmaus community is invited to participate in the Candlelight service, which is preceded by Holy Communion for the Emmaus community.

CHRYSALIS: The youth/young adult version of The Walk to Emmaus, designed for older high-school students and college-age young adults.

CLOSING: A ceremony at the end of the three-day event in which pilgrims are united with the Emmaus community, which greets them and welcomes them into the ongoing life of the Emmaus community in their area.

CURSILLO: *Cursillo de Cristianidad* (Spanish for "short course in Christianity") is the predecessor to The Walk to Emmaus. Having originated in the Roman Catholic Church, Cursillo now has expressions in other faith traditions as well.

DAY FOUR: All the days that follow one's three-day Walk to Emmaus.

EMMAUS COMMUNITY: The gathering of all who have partici-pated in an Emmaus weekend in a given locale for the purpose of rekindling the spirit and friendship of their weekends.

GROUP REUNION: A small group of Christian friends who meet to discuss piety, study, and action — three aspects of the Christian life. Members of these groups encourage and challenge one another in their discipleship.

LAY DIRECTOR: The primary layperson who directs the activities during the Emmaus weekend.

PILGRIM: One who has participated in The Walk to Emmaus.

SEND-OFF: The gathering of sponsors, team members, and prospective pilgrims that begins the 72-hour Walk to Emmaus.

SPIRITUAL DIRECTOR: A clergyperson in residence who guides pilgrims in their journey during The Walk to Emmaus, leads worship services, and gives talks on the nature and experience of grace.

SPONSORS' HOUR: A brief service of prayer in which sponsors covenant their support of the pilgrims during The Walk to Emmaus. It is held immediately after Send-Off.

TALKS: The presentation of the core elements of the short course in Christianity. The Upper Room provides talk outlines (for both clergy and lay talks) to give the framework of the talks for The Walk to Emmaus.

WALK TO EMMAUS: A three-day walk with Jesus Christ. It is a short course in the scripture and vital piety that leads to a lifetime of Christian discipleship.

72-HOUR PRAYER VIGIL: An organized vigil from 7:00 P.M. Thursday until 7:00 P.M. Sunday. Members of the local Emmaus community pray constantly during this time for the pilgrims' openness to the inpouring of God's grace in their lives.

APPENDIX 2

SUGGESTED READING

> To order resources in this section,
> call (800) 972-0433 Monday through Friday, or
> visit us online at www.upperroom.org/bookstore.
> Except where noted, resources are also available
> through Cokesbury bookstores.

The following Emmaus resources are available only from Upper Room Ministries Customer Service Department.

Emmaus brochures, package of 100 (#16)

Chrysalis brochures, package of 100 (#22)

Introduction to Walk to Emmaus video (#40)

The Emmaus Library Series

What Is Emmaus? by Stephen D. Bryant—Answers the most frequently asked questions about Emmaus, the Emmaus community, and Emmaus follow-up groups. #881

The Group Reunion by Stephen D. Bryant—Designed for persons who have participated in The Walk to Emmaus, this booklet contains guidance on the spiritual purpose and practices of the group reunion. #884

Coming Down from the Mountain: Returning to Your Congregation by Lawrence Martin—To help pilgrims make the transition back to their congregations, this booklet includes fun and informative chapters such as "Long-Term Obedience in a Single Direction," "Agape Unplugged," and "On Not Being an Emmaus Groupie." #882

Spiritual Directors by Kay Gray—Addresses the role of Spiritual Directors; the qualifications for selection; and their responsibilities before, during, and after the three days. #886

Spiritual Growth through Team Experience by Joanne Bultemeier—This booklet explains qualities of a team member, spiritual benefits of team membership, what happens at team meetings, and leadership development. #885

The Board of Directors by Richard A. Gilmore—This insightful resource covers responsibilities of board members, duties of the board committees, possible committee assignments, and more. #883

Walking Side by Side: Devotions for Pilgrims by Joanne Bultemeier and Cherie Jones—Forty-five meditations based on the fifteen talks given during The Walk offer an excellent way to continue spiritual disciplines of daily prayer and meditation. #880

Sponsorship by Richard and Janine Gilmore—The Gilmores guide individuals through the process of sponsoring fellow pilgrims by exploring the range of possibilities in the role of the sponsor for the renewal of church leaders, Emmaus communities, and the church. #873

Music Directors by Sandy Stickney—Stickney describes the importance of music in the Emmaus experience, offering practical insights on topics ranging from ego to copyright requirements. Written with humor, directness, and a spirit of servanthood. #911

The Early History of The Walk to Emmaus by Robert Wood—The founding international director of The Walk to Emmaus gives a firsthand account of the beginnings of the movement. In addition to a timeline of significant events in the Emmaus movement, Wood also writes about Chrysalis, the youth/ young adult expression of Emmaus. #962

**The following books on spiritual formation
may help you in your Fourth Day.**

Piety

The Christ-Centered Woman: Finding Balance in a World of Extremes
by Kimberly Dunnam Reisman—By unmasking dangerous
stereotypes and common traps women may fall into, Reisman
offers women ways to identify their true selves as disciples
and tells how to place Christ at the center of their lives. #913

Creating a Life with God: The Call of Ancient Prayer Practices by Daniel
Wolpert—Historical figures guide readers through twelve
prayer practices. Wolpert offers step-by-step instructions for
each practice. #9855

Dimensions of Prayer: Cultivating a Relationship with God by Douglas
V. Steere—In a new format of his classic book, Steere suggests
that we begin to pray by acknowledging our dependence on a
God of love and power; then we move on to more practical
aspects of prayer, which he explores with wit and insight. #971

Fire in the Soul: A Prayer Book for the Later Years by Richard L.
Morgan—This prayer book helps older adults seek God's help
in meeting late-life challenges. Morgan draws on his own personal prayers as well as classic prayers from John Calvin,
Saint Augustine, John Donne, and Teresa of Avila. #879

A Guide to Prayer for All God's People by Norman Shawchuck and
Rueben P. Job—Offers selected scriptures, formal prayers,
and thematic readings that provide the structure for daily
meditations and monthly personal retreats. #710

A Guide to Prayer for All Who Seek God by Rueben P. Job and
Norman Shawchuck—Follows the Christian year and the
lectionary readings; each day offers guidance for an opening
affirmation, a petition of prayer, a scripture selection, and
excerpts from Christian classics as well as more recently
published works. #999

Heart Whispers: Benedictine Wisdom for Today by Elizabeth J.
Canham—*Heart Whispers* translates the basics of sixth-century

Benedictine spirituality to help us live spiritually abundant lives in today's stressful world. Readers will discover anew that life with God is a journey that grows richer and more blessed in response to God's grace. #892 (Leader's guide: #893)

Journeying Through the Days: A Calendar and Journal for Personal Reflection (annual publication) — Contains daily scripture selections from a variety of translations, inspirational quotations, and ample space for journaling. A natural companion to *The Upper Room Disciplines.*

Journeymen by Kent Ira Groff—*Journeymen* encourages readers to make the connection between being men and being Christians, integrating the feeling of power and the power of feeling. Exploring men's particular wounds and the promise of healing through Christ, *Journeymen* offers biblical examples, the author's own stories and those of other men, prayer exercises, meditations, and reflection questions. #862

A Life-Shaping Prayer: 52 Meditations in the Wesleyan Spirit by Paul Wesley Chilcote—Elizabeth Rhodes, an early Wesley follower, was transformed in her spiritual disciplines by committing to memory a prayer that became an unusual blessing. She prayed for a "waking spirit, and a diligent soul."#9938

Openings: A Daybook of Saints, Psalms, and Prayers by Larry James Peacock—Each daily reading features a notable person of faith or significant event, a psalm, a time to ponder on the scripture or person of faith, and suggestions for a particular Christian prayer practice. #9850

Quiet Spaces: Prayer Interludes for Women by Patricia Wilson—This book offers women short prayer interludes amid the busyness of their daily schedules. Wilson helps women discover the quiet moments that help them connect with God. Each prayer interlude has five parts: calming, centering, praying, listening, and returning. #969

Talking in the Dark: Praying When Life Doesn't Make Sense by Steve Harper—No matter how lost readers may feel, Harper assures them that they are not wanderers in life's trackless desert but pilgrims through prayer's wilderness of mystery and grace. #9922

Teach Me to Pray by W. E. Sangster — This classic on the essence of Christianity has helped millions of Christians around the world. Sangster addresses practical questions about prayer, urges readers to form prayer groups or prayer cells, and discusses ways to "live in Christ" and give our hearts and minds to Christian discipleship. #125

Traveling the Prayer Paths of Jesus by John Indermark — Join Jesus in places of prayer and learn from daily readings that examine Jesus' prayers in six very different settings: out of solitude, by the roadside, on the mountainside, in the upper room, at the garden, and upon the cross. #9857

The Upper Room Disciplines: A Book of Daily Devotions (annual publication) — Join writers, pastors, preachers, scholars, and a worldwide ecumenical community in integrating the scriptures into your daily life. Each week a fresh voice guides readers through the daily scripture readings, practicing the spiritual disciplines of Bible reading, reflection, and prayer.

The Workbook of Living Prayer (20th Anniversary Edition) by Maxie Dunnam — This workbook teaches readers to pray in a simple, practical way. Updated and revised, this six-week personal adventure in prayer will strengthen a new generation of pray-ers as well as those who have used it before. #718

Study

Do What You Have the Power to Do by Helen Bruch Pearson—This book is a Bible study based on six familiar stories of encounters between Jesus and unnamed women. The six-week study challenges Christians to develop and invest their gifts and talents to move church and society closer to the community Jesus envisioned. #643

Genesis of Grace: A Lenten Book of Days by John Indermark—This book leads readers to a deeper understanding of God's grace by tracing it through the familiar stories of Genesis. Daily reflective readings explore the theme of God's forgiveness as revealed in such stories as the Creation, the Flood, Cain and Abel, and Abraham and Sarah. #843 (Leader's guide: #844)

Get Real: A Spiritual Journey for Men by Derek Maul—Maul delivers straight talk about faith, family, and desire for God. A serious Christian life requires getting hungry for God, giving up shallow priorities, and finding joy in simple service to others; in other words, getting real. #9911 (Leader's guide, #9924)

One Day at a Time: Discovering the Freedom of 12-Step Spirituality by Trevor Hudson—Hudson writes this book for those who worry too much, struggle with compulsive or addictive behavior, battle with stress and tension. Working the 12 Steps can become God's way of keeping life on track. #9913

The Power of a Focused Heart: 8 Life Lessons from the Beatitudes by Mary Lou Redding—Five exercises per week help readers apply scripture to their lives. The book offers helps for decision making based on readers' spiritual gifts. #9818

Remember Who You Are: Baptism, a Model for Christian Life by William H. Willimon—Designed for those who are searching for the meaning of baptism, this book explores the significance of this sacrament in daily life and provides a model for Christian living. A study guide for small groups is included. #399

Servants, Misfits, and Martyrs: Saints and Their Stories by James C. Howell—Discover a world of saints whose faith, hope, and action will inspire and encourage you: Francis of Assisi,

Clarence Jordan, Billy Graham, Sojourner Truth, Charles Wesley, Isaac Watts, John Newton, Dorothy Day, and others. This book introduces readers to ordinary people who led exemplary lives by giving themselves to God. #906

Shaped by the Word: The Power of Scripture in Spiritual Formation, revised edition by M. Robert Mulholland Jr. — In exploring the role scripture plays in spiritual formation, Mulholland examines obstacles we often encounter in spiritual reading and introduces a new way of study that enlivens the scriptures. #936

Stretch Out Your Hand: Exploring Healing Prayer by Tilda Norberg and Robert D. Webber — *Stretch Out Your Hand* suggests that healing is not just getting well from an illness but a beautiful dynamic process leading to the wholeness God wills for us. The authors offer practical ways for readers to consider the varieties of God's healing love and look at difficult questions about prayer and the role of faith in healing. #872 (Leader's guide: #871)

Sunday Dinner: The Lord's Supper and the Christian Life by William H. Willimon — This book is for those who want to explore the meaning of the gift of the Lord's Supper and its significance for their daily lives as Christians. #429

The Upper Room Spiritual Classics, Series 1, Compiled and introduced by Keith Beasley-Topliffe — Excerpts from the writings of Augustine, John Wesley, John Cassian, Thomas Kelly, and Teresa of Avila. #832

The Upper Room Spiritual Classics, Series 2. Compiled and introduced by Keith Beasley-Topliffe — Excerpts from the writings of Julian of Norwich, Francis and Clare of Assisi, Thomas à Kempis, Evelyn Underhill, and Toyohiko Kagawa. #853

The Upper Room Spiritual Classics, Series 3, Compiled and introduced by Keith Beasley-Topliffe — Excerpts from the writings of the desert mothers and fathers, John of the Cross, Catherine of Siena, William Law, and John Woolman. #905

The Workbook of Intercessory Prayer by Maxie Dunnam — This seven-week study guide gives participants an opportunity to experience the impact prayer can make on others' lives. #382

The Workbook on Becoming Alive in Christ by Maxie Dunnam—In this seven-week study, Dunnam helps readers experience the indwelling Christ as the shaping power for their lives. #542

The Workbook on the Christian Walk by Maxie Dunnam—In this seven-week study, readers study the importance of Christian action as they strive to walk faithfully with Christ. #640

The Workbook on Keeping Company with the Saints by Maxie Dunnam—Draw from the rich well of the writings of the saints as Maxie Dunnam guides you in a seven-week study on the lives and teachings of William Law, Julian of Norwich, Brother Lawrence, and Teresa of Avila. #925

The Workbook on Lessons from the Saints by Maxie Dunnam—In this eight-week study, Dunnam suggests how Christians can grow spiritually by learning from earlier generations of Christians. He draws insights from a group of saints that include Martin Luther, John Wesley, Francis de Sales, Margery Kempe, Francis of Assisi, and Thérèse of Lisieux. #965

The Workbook on Spiritual Disciplines by Maxie Dunnam—Dunnam says that the purpose of discipline for Christians is spiritual growth and the renewal of their minds. This six-week study helps participants make their lives more effective, meaningful, and joyful. #479

The Workbook on the Seven Deadly Sins by Maxie Dunnam and Kimberly Dunnam Reisman—This eight-week study focuses on the traditional categories of personal sin and illustrates how sloth, lust, anger, pride, envy, gluttony, and greed are ever present in our lives and in society. Participants in this study will learn how Christ can bring deliverance and new growth. #714

The Workbook on Virtues and the Fruit of the Spirit by Maxie Dunnam and Kimberly Dunnam Reisman—By looking at the seven cardinal virtues and the fruit of the Spirit, this study leads participants to be the persons they were created to be. #854

Wrestling with Grace: A Spirituality for the Rough Edges of Daily Life
by Robert Corin Morris — Offering new insights into the daily
practice of Christian spirituality, this book takes readers on a
personal journey to see the possibilities of grace. A how-to
manual about loving yourself, others, the world around you,
and God, especially on the "Thursday afternoons" of life,
when the going gets tough. #985

Action

And Not One Bird Stopped Singing: Coping with Transition and Loss in Aging by Doris Moreland Jones—Whereas society encourages us to ignore the emotions that accompany loss, Jones helps us cope honestly with feelings of loss in death, in diminishing body function, and in other experiences related to aging. #815

Children and Prayer: A Shared Pilgrimage by Betty Shannon Cloyd—Written by a Christian educator and diaconal minister, this book helps parents and caregivers enrich the prayer lives of children. Cloyd provides prayers and rituals to use with children and answers the difficult questions children (and adults) often ask about God. #803

Discovering Community: A Meditation on Community in Christ by Stephen V. Doughty—What does it mean when we say we are part of the community of Christ? Doughty focuses on the diverse ways and places in which Christian disciples grow— in community. #870

In the Shadow of God's Wings: Grace in the Midst of Depression by Susan Gregg-Schroeder—In taking us on her personal journey into depression, Gregg-Schroeder encourages a new understanding of the spiritual gifts that can come from depression. #807 (Leader's guide: #859)

The Jesus Priorities: 8 Essential Habits by Christopher Maricle— "What would Jesus do?" is the guiding question for living the Christian life. Maricle maps out the main priorities that Jesus modeled in his life and ministry. #9914

Kindred Souls: Connecting Through Spiritual Friendship by Stephanie Ford—What is spiritual friendship? How can readers find kindred souls on the spiritual journey? Ford answers these and other questions. #9903

Parents and Grandparents As Spiritual Guides: Nurturing Children of the Promise by Betty Shannon Cloyd—Cloyd explores simple ways parents and grandparents can introduce children to the presence of God and nurture them spiritually during daily, routine activities. This must-have book includes biblical models of spiritual guides, along with insightful stories from children, Christian educators, and the author's own family experience. #923

Prayer, Stress, and Our Inner Wounds by Flora Slosson Wuellner— In describing various kinds of pain, Wuellner offers practical ways that prayer can help us find inner healing. God's grace moves through this caring book to work in the lives of readers as they confront their own needs and pain. #501

Rediscovering Our Spiritual Gifts: Building Up the Body of Christ through the Gifts of the Spirit by Charles V. Bryant—Bryant offers an objective and positive approach to discovering our spiritual gifts and provides an inventory to help readers name and apply the gifts in their own lives. #633

Remembering Your Story: Creating Your Own Spiritual Autobiography (Revised Edition) by Richard L. Morgan—Morgan guides readers to understand and share their spiritual stories, weaving insights from evangelism, Bible study, family therapy, pastoral care, gerontology, spiritual direction, and theology. His work guides readers to deeper memories of God's presence in all parts of life. #963 (Leader's guide: #964)

Selecting Church Leaders: A Practice in Spiritual Discernment by Chuck Olsen and Ellen Morseth—The authors offer a spiritually solid approach to selecting church leaders; they believe that spiritual guidance is often missing in the selection process of leaders. They urge readers to participate in a prayerful process of seeking God's yearning, whether for an individual, a local church, or a denomination. #961

The Soul of Tomorrow's Church by Kent Ira Groff—The author invites congregational leaders to weave spiritual practices into all aspects of ministry. The soul of tomorrow's church will be restored as spiritual practices are woven into five ministry functions: worship, administration, education, soul care, and outreach. Each chapter teems with practical ways to weave spiritual practices of prayer, discernment, faith stories, silence, and hospitality into each of these five ministry functions. #927

Transforming Ventures: A Spiritual Guide for Volunteers in Mission by Jane Ives — With a strong emphasis on scripture, personal witness, and spiritual practices, *Transforming Ventures* provides for spiritual reflection and growth while people serve in short-term mission. #910

Walking through the Waters: Biblical Reflections for Families of Cancer Patients by Nancy Regensburger — Grounded in scripture, this book offers gentle spiritual guidance to families and friends living with cancer. Drawing from her husband's battle with lymphoma, the author demonstrates that being attentive to one's spiritual life in the midst of illness can bring comfort and healing. In 15 personal reflections, Regensburger tells what was meaningful for her and guides readers in ways to sense God's presence during times of uncertainty. #934

Yours Are the Hands of Christ by James C. Howell — Christians long to make a difference in the world as a faithful response to the call of discipleship. *Yours Are the Hands of Christ* helps readers find ways to apply their faith in daily life. This book takes a fresh look at familiar moments in Jesus' life and draws on the lives of saints throughout history who model how to be the hands of Christ today. #867

Don't miss these magazines published by The Upper Room. For individual subscriptions, call toll-free 1-800-925-6847. For group bulk orders, call toll-free 1-800-972-0433.

Alive Now—Each bimonthly issue includes themes that follow the seasons of the church year. The magazine seeks to nourish people who hunger for a sacred way of living in today's world. Contains contributions from well-known authors such as Anne Lamott, daily devotions, interviews with contemporary thinkers, and award-winning poetry. A new feature, "Taking It Further," draws from books, films, and the Internet.

Devo'Zine (for youth, ages 12–17)—This devotional magazine is written by youth and those who love them. The devotions address real-life issues teens face every day, helping them establish a lifelong practice of spending time with God and of reflecting on what God is doing in their lives.

El Aposento Alto (Spanish version of *The Upper Room* daily devotional guide)—*El Aposento Alto* es la guía devocional de mayor circulación en el mundo entero. Esta guía le ayudará a fortalecer su fe por medio de meditaciones llenas de profundo significado personal, escritas por los propios lectores. Diariamente se incluye un verisículo bíblico; se ofrece una meditación, una oración, un motivo de oración y un pensamienta para el día.

Pockets (for children ages 6–12)—This devotional magazine is filled with stories, activities, games, daily scripture readings, and more. Along with all the fun comes the encouragement for children to form a habit of daily prayer, Bible reading, and journaling.

The Upper Room daily devotional guide—Reader-written meditations share the heartfelt spiritual experiences of Christians from around the world. *The Upper Room* is a perfect companion for individuals, family devotional time, and small-group study.

Weavings: A Journal of the Christian Spiritual Life—Offers an ever-deepening experience of God and a fresh perspective on the Christian faith, weaving together the immediacy of personal experience and the enduring truths of scripture. Issues contain articles, scripture meditations, and book reviews.